D1086725

ALL DAY PERMANENT RED

by the same author

poetry
SELECTED POEMS
WAR MUSIC:
An Account of Books 1–4 and 16–19
of Homer's *Iliad*

prose
PRINCE CHARMING: A MEMOIR

ALL DAY
PERMANENT RED

The first battle scenes
of Homer's *Iliad* rewritten
PART ONE

CHRISTOPHER LOGUE

faber and faber

First published in 2003
by Faber and Faber Limited
3 Queen Square London WC1N 3AU
Published in the United States by Faber and Faber Inc.
an affiliate of Farrar, Straus and Giroux LLC, New York

Photoset by Wilmaset Ltd, Wirral
Printed in England by T J International Ltd, Padstow, Cornwall

All rights reserved
© Christopher Logue, 2003

The right of Christopher Logue to be identified as author
of this work has been asserted in accordance with Section 77
of the Copyright, Designs and Patents Act 1988

All performing rights in this work are fully protected and
permission to perform it in whole or in part must be obtained
in advance from David Godwin Associates, 55 Monmouth Street,
London WC2H 9DG, or from Faber and Faber Limited

Audiologue, a seven-CD set of recordings by Christopher Logue
that includes the full text of *War Music*, is available from
Unknown Public Limited, Suite 8, Grove House, London W10H 5BZ

*This book is sold subject to the condition that it shall not,
by way of trade or otherwise, be lent, resold, hired out or
otherwise circulated without the publisher's prior consent
in any form of binding or cover other than that in which it
is published and without a similar condition including this
condition being imposed on the subsequent purchaser*

A CIP record for this book
is available from the British Library

ISBN 0–571–21686–2

2 4 6 8 10 9 7 5 3 1

ACKNOWLEDGEMENTS

To Craig Raine who edited the text, and to Liane Aukin who commented on it; to Charles Boyle who copy-edited, and to Mildred Marney who processed it; to my agent David Godwin, and to my publisher, Matthew Evans.

Parts of the text have appeared in *Areté*, the *Threepenny Review* and the *Times Literary Supplement*.

ALL DAY PERMANENT RED

Slope. Strip. Slope.
Right. Centre. Left.
Road. Track. Cross.
Ridge. Plain. Sea.

Go back an hour.
See what the Mousegod saw.

Two slopes
Brilliantly lit
Double the width of Troy
Divided by a strip

30 yards wide.

The gentler, longer slope, that leads
Via its ridge onto the Trojan plain
Is occupied by 50,000 Greeks
Silent behind their masks, yearning to fight

But not until:
'Now!'
'Now!'

Hector emerges and commits the Ilian host
Their coffin-topped rhinoceros and oxhide shields
Packing the counter-slope

And presently the Skéan Gate is closed.

Out on the Panachéan right
Some cross-slope skirmishing.

The Trojan centre has begun to edge onto the strip.

The ridge.
King Agamemnon views Troy's skyline.

Windmills. Palms.

'It will be ours by dark.'

Not far from him, concerned
That in this final action those they lead
Should fight and fight and fight again,
The hero lords:

Nestor, his evening star.
His silent fortress, Ajax. Good – even on soft sand.
Odysseus (you know him), small but big.
Fourth – grizzled and hook-tap nosed – the king of Crete,
        Idomeneo, who:
    'Come on!'
Would sign a five-war-contract on the nod.

The Gate – still closed.

Across the strip
Lord Panda spots a Greek called Quist, and says:

'Watch this,' to his admirer Biblock as
He beckons up his oriental bow.

Then a shield hid Quist.

'Biblock, my father manufactures chariots.
I have a dozen. Lovely things.
I cannot bear to lose my horses in this war.
No mind. My motto is: *Start the day well*. An early kill.
It gets one in the mood.
    You know it was my shot that saved the war?'
    'I know it, Panda. Yes.'
    'However Biblock, mood, important though it is, is –'
Tapping his temple '– worthless minus brains.'

The armies hum
As power-station outflow cables do.
    The Trojan's edge.
The light goes upright through the sky.
    Downslope,
Child Diomed to those who follow him:

    'Still.'
    'Still.'

The King: 'I know Prince Hector. We will strike
When, as he always does, he stops to incite his host.'

Odysseus and Bombax have gone down
Slope-centre to their Ithacans.

The Trojans jeer: 'No fight!' and edge.

The Child:

'Still...'
'Still...'

'Biblock, my eyes are alpha.
But what your brain takes from your sight
Before it tells your biceps what to do, is key.
When the fighting starts you stick by me.
See brainwork work, not what the stars foretell.'
Which was, unluckily, what Biblock did.
   'Hold on, there is that Greek.'
And there was Quist.

To the sigh of the string, see Panda's shot float off;
To the slap of the string on the stave, float on
Over the strip for a beat, a beat; and then
Carry a tunnel the width of a lipstick through Quist's neck.

The Skéan Gate swings up.

Nothing will happen until Hector exits.

There is a touch of thunder in the west.

He does.

Odysseus: 'Thank God.'

Idomeneo: 'And about time, too.'

And, save for the edgers-on along the strip,
Prince Hector's thousands turn;
Then genuflect; then whisper:

6

'Now ...'

'Now ...'

'Now ...'

Go close.

Besides his helmet and his loincloth Hector wore
A battle-skirt of silver mesh,
Its band, a needlepoint procession:
Sangárian tigers, each with a lifted paw.

The Gate swings down.

On either forearm as on either shin
Lightweight self-sprung wraparound guards
Decked with a slash of yellow chrome without
Dotted with silver knots and stars within.
And now –
As he moves through the light
Downwards along the counterslope, his shield,
Whose rim's ceramic fold will shatter bronze
Whose 16 alternating gold and silver radiants
Burst from an adamant medusa-Aphrodité boss
(Its hair bouffant with venomous eels
The pupils of its bullet-starred-glass eyes
Catching the sun) catching the sun
Chylábborak, Aeneas and Anáxapart,
Quibuph, Kykéon, Akafáct and Palt
Cantering their chariots to the right of his,
His silver mittens up (a perfect fit,
They go with everything)

Sarpédon, Gray, Bárbarinth, Hágnet, Ábassee,
His favourite brother,
Cantering their chariots to his left:

    'Still...'

    'Still...'

    Lutie, his nephew, this-day's driver ('fast and safe')
Catching his eye, flicking the horses on –
    On either side of him,
Beating their spears against their coffin-tops.
His army parts.

    And now the Lord of Light filled Hector's voice
– Him moving on, on, forwards, down, towards the strip –
With certainty.
    And descant to his thousands:
    'Now!'
    'Now!'
    'Now!'
That full, clear voice, rose like an arrow through the air:

    'Are you ready to fight?'
    'We are!'
    'Are you happy to kill?'
    'We are!'
    'Are you willing to die?'
    'Yes!'
    'Yes!'
    'Then bind to me! I am your Prince!
In my command you will win fame!
The victory is God's!'

On hearing this,
To welcome Hector to his death
God sent a rolling thunderclap across the sky
The city and the sea
        And momentarily –
The breezes playing with the sunlit dust –
On either slope a silence fell.

Think of a raked sky-wide Venetian blind.
Add the receding traction of its slats
Of its slats of its slats as a hand draws it up.
Hear the Greek army getting to its feet:

Then of a stadium when many boards are raised
And many faces change to one vast face.
So, where there were so many masks,
Now one Greek mask glittered from strip to ridge.

Already swift
Boy Lutie took Prince Hector's nod
And fired his whip that right and left
Signalled to Ilium's wheels to fire their own,
And to the Wall-wide nodding plumes of Trojan infantry –

Flutes!
Flutes!
Screeching above the grave percussion of their feet
Shouting how they will force the savage Greeks
Back up the slope over the ridge, downplain
And slaughter them beside their ships –

Add the reverberation of their hooves: and
    'Reach for your oars...'
T'lespiax, his yard at 60°, sending it
Across the radiant air as Ilium swept

Onto the strip
Into the Greeks
Over the venue where
Two hours ago all present prayed for peace.
    And carried Greece
Back up the slope that leads
    Via its ridge
    Onto the windy plain.

Dispersed across its middle left
Extended lines of shields collide, totter apart
Shuffle back shouting in their ankle dust
Turning from lines to crescents, crescents to shorter lines
Backstepping into circles, or
Parties just wandering about aimlessly.

    And through their intervals,
Now moving, pausing now, now moving on,
His court – their comet's tail of wheel-dust – close behind,
Swift through the gorgeous light, Lutie on reins,
Lord of the Chariots, Hector's chariot goes
Racing across the left but seen
As the Mousegod wants him to be seen
As everywhere at once.

    Right now near Hyacinth the son of Hyacinth, a Greek
Able to quarry slate, throw a fair pot (and decorate it)
He chose to follow Agamemnon (still up-ridge
Still saying 'Ours by dark...') while Hyacinth stood
Alone in the dispersal, awed
By Hector's speed by Hector's light as Hector jumped
His sword – that caught the light – into his other hand

Lent out across the Troyside wheel
And wishing him the very best of luck
Decapitated Hyacinth as they passed
On, out, far left, U-turned beside Sarpédon, saying:
    'Dear Intrepidity,
Mark time until I tell T'lespiax to signal the advance.'
    Nodded to Gray, to Bárbarinth, told Palt –
The dearest of his court – to strip the headless Greek
And take his bronze-wear back to Troy
(Which Palt part did) then waved to them
As Lutie cracked his pair along the track that runs
Parallel to the strip, towards the middle of the slope.

Go there.

The situation is unpromising.

Spanning the track
Some half-way up between the ridge/the strip
Fenced in behind their shields
2000 masks around Odysseus.
    Surrounding them lord Ábassee
With more.
    And over there
Coming down-track towards those roundabouts,
Hector and Lutie's dust.

    See Coriot and Shell
Ithacan hunters bred on Mount Neritos.
    Some said bare-chested Artemis
God of all animals bar us

Had taught these brothers how to ride and shoot.
She did not help them now.

   Running the horses off their chariot's shaft
They galloped, leapt the shields – and Bombax: 'No!' –
Knees in bows up straight at the coffin-tops
And never saw Lord Hector sign: 'Between...'
Or Lutie swerve off-track and put –
Now at full height gauging his cast, his shield
Sweeping Shell's bowshot wide – his Prince
Exactly where he asked. Who cast, and oh my God
As Hector's spear entered Shell's abdomen
The arrow's ricochet hit Coriot in the eye
And off he came, and died. As Shell,
Screaming, was bolted by his frightened horse
Into the Trojan coffin-tops
Where, axe up, Ábassee's minder, Dial, (with
The sound that a butcher's chopper makes
As it goes through a carcass into his block)
Finished him off.

   Long afterwards it was recalled
That Sheepgrove, Ithaca's adopted son,
Made sure that Shell and Coriot's parents got
The ashes of their twins, their only sons.
Therefore their high-roofed house
Above its wall of winding rock in distant Ithaca
Went to a farming aunt. While Palt,
Lost to the fame combat alone can bring,
Ignored (again) Hector's: 'Return the bodies of those two.'
Told Meep (his man) to see to it
And followed Hector back along the slope.

Headlock. Body slam. Hands that do not reach back. Low dust.
Stormed by Chylábborak, driven-in by Ábassee
The light above his circle hatched with spears
Odysseus to Sheepgrove:

'Get lord Idomeneo from the ridge.'

Then prays:

'Brainchild Athena, Holy Girl,
As one you made
As calm and cool as water in well.
I know that you have cares enough
Other than those of me and mine.
Yet, Daughter of God, without your help
We cannot last.'

Setting down her topaz saucer heaped with nectarine jelly
Emptying her blood-red mouth set in her ice-white face
Teenaged Athena jumped up and shrieked:
   'Kill! Kill for me!
Better to die than to live without killing!'

Who says prayer does no good?

Seeing Athena's cry raise fight and fire in lord Odysseus,
Hera, Heaven's creamy Queen, told Diomed
(Still near the strip, content amid the crackle of snapped spears):

'Odysseus needs you. Go.'

Beneath a rise
300 paces downslope from
Chylábborak and Ábassee
A party of 500 wandering Greeks
See Hector parked and praying:

'Lord of Light . . .'

While Lutie fills a bucket from the well
Where the Skean road that runs from Troy
Straight up the slope to the ridge
Crosses the track.

'. . . I shall be busy until dark.
If I forget you, do not you, me.'

Out from the wanderers the Teucer boys
Iólo, 16, from a wife, and Párthenos
Bred from a she Teucer inherited
Come crouch-down hurrying convinced that this
Their chance for fame Prince Hector dead etc has come.
Párthenos set to plant his spear by Hector's spine,
Iólo, well . . .

Boy Lutie is astonished by their impudence
But not enough to not, in one,
Put down the bucket thrash his whip, its crack
Recalling Hector to his fate, its tip – as Párthenos
Jumped for the chariot's tailgate
And Hector's mittened hand snaffles his wispy beard –
Circling Iólo's wrist.

Párthenos kisses Hector's wrist.
His eyes are full of words.

'Take a deep breath before you speak, Greek boy.'

He does.

'Please, Prince of the Gate, take us alive.
We did not want to come to Troy.
We could not disobey our father's words.
His mother was your aunt Hesíone.
He has a wall of swords –'
    'With silver hilts,' Iólo says –
'And gold – a chest of gold.
Please. Please. Please. Please.'

The wanderers edge in.

Hector steps down.
The Teucer boys may not have been the brightest on the slope
But they are bright enough to know death when they see it.
    'Keep your lives,' he said. 'A gift from Troy.'
And as they ran, made
    'Go' to Lutie with his head,
Studied the wanderers,
Lifted the bucket, doused himself
And charged.

See an East African lion
    Nose tip to tail tuft ten, eleven feet
    Slouching towards you
    Swaying its head from side to side
    Doubling its pace, its gold-black mane
    That stretches down its belly to its groin
    Catching the sunlight as it hits
    Twice its own length a beat, then leaps
    Great forepaws high great claws disclosed
    The scarlet insides of its mouth

Parting a roar as loud as sail-sized flames
And lands, slam-scattering the herd.

'That is how Hector came on us.'

Despite the few who ran
Out from the rest to get at him and died
Or ducked and dodged his restless spear
And came away covered with blood and died,
Like shoppers trapped by a calamity
The rest pressed back onto the rest.
And he, partly to please his comet's tail,
Took sideway jumps – one foot up to the other in the air –
Chattering his spear along their front.

The ridge.

Sheepgrove (as asked).

Idomeneo does not wait.

Dustlight. Far off
A woman with an infant on her back
Is picking fruit.

Enter the Child.

Be advised,
If you cannot give death the two-finger-flip
Do not fight by or against Queen Hera's human
The son of Tydéus murderous Diomed aka the Child.

Tall. Blond. With a huge nose and lots of corkscrew curls.
Followed as he springs off his chariot's plate by 50 masks
And tells the wanderers
(As Séthynos, his heart, his next, springs down):
    'Your lord has come.'
Shoulders his way towards their front:
    'Honour him with your lives.'
Steps through:
    'Ave!'
Sees Hector far down front. Sees Palt
His Porsche-fine chariot with Meep on reins
Arriving with the comet's tail.

    Palt was a kind, religious man,
Loving his Prince and loved by him.
Most days in pre-war days saw many guests
Around Palt's pool. But now, at 45,
Seeking the fame combat alone can bring
He chose to fight.
    Some said that God
Who recognises hospitality
Would save His worshipper – but no.

    As Palt and Meep tried to jump down,
Too far to stop it Hector saw the Child
Who did not break his stride
Or seem to notice them especially
Reverse his spear bash out Meep's eyes
Then re-reversing, plunge –
Mid-jump, with sword part drawn –
Its 18-inch bronze tooth
(That caught the light) into Palt's side:
And as premechanised harvesters their sheaves
Pitch him in dreadful pain sideways across his pair
Into the dust at Hector's feet.

Blind as the Cyclops with fraternal tears
Prince Hector prayed:

'God, stifle my grief,
And bless my plan –'

Which is:
To pull Odysseus' thousands (and now Diomed)
Onto himself, and hold them there, while signalling
The left and right wings of the slope
(Sarpédon's Lycians, Aeneas' Dardanelles)
To advance, turn inwards, meet, and so divide
The mid-slope from the ridgeline Greeks.

– Then stopped and put the Child between himself
And Palt, now on his hands and knees,
Holding the slick blue-greenish loops of his intestines up
Though some were dragging in the dust.
   Diomed telling Séthynos:
   'Finish him. Then strip that showcase plate.'
Taking a step towards Hector, who moved back
As Palt choked out:
   'Friend, I am gone.
I beg you not to leave the thing I was as dog-meat for the Greeks.'
   This
As Séthynos unlatched
And jerked his bloodsmeared urn off
While those behind the Child jeered:
   'Troy on a drip!'
As kind Palt died,
   And Hector, dogged by Diomed,
Hovered some paces off, hearing him shout,
Seeing his masks begin to butcher Palt:
   'Prince, by the light of Troy alight
Our herd will share what we Greek heroes left.'

'Yes!'
'Yes!'
'Who else can stop it if
Hector, the irreplaceable Trojan, lacks
The guts to guard the body of his friend?'

'Silence that liar with a single blow,' was Hector's thought
Though to Chylábborak and Ábassee he said:
    'Fall back three spearcasts to the rise above the well.'

From time to time
Here on the agricultural
And poppy-dotted districts of the right-hand slope
Aeneas' thousands occupy, his lords
Lighting each other's pipes beside their wheels
Reckon the battle has as battles do
Found its own voice, that, presently far off
Blends with the sound of clear bright water as it falls
Over their covert's mossy heights;
A peaceful dust-free place circled by poplar trees,
Good cover and green shade.

    Aeneas often sits apart.
He has his mother's face: white skin, green eyes,
A slow, unbroken look. And though there is
A touch too much of satisfaction in his confidence
As with the Prince your eyes incline to him.

    'Ah . . .' standing '. . . Lutie.'

Sending for Panda and Achátes.

'Sire... ...move when you hear T'lespiax' *Advance.*'
And he was gone.

Slope centre. Hear the Child
Shouting the shouts of an heroic lord:

'Strike for the face! The seat of the soul!'

Beseeching Hera as he ran
(That Queen so happy for herself and him):

'Blest Sister Wife of God
Give me the might and courage to become
The killer of the day.'

The masks behind him baying:
'Troy for us!'
Her power surging through him, he
Cast as he leapt at them; barbecued three;
Crashed through their coffin-tops;
Gaffed this plume dead; cut fillets out of those;
His masks behind him through the gap
Him making for the rise topped by Prince Hector's vulture
plume.

Consider how, when sought,
The cliff-head whales that frequent
The sunlit radius of Antarctica
Tail down beneath its fields of rustling ice
Then 30 minutes later raise
Their rainbow spouts above a far lagoon.

So Hector trapped the Child, who made no mind
S-curving through these Trojans; hammering those;
As many arrows on his posy shield
As microphones on politicians' stands:

'I fight my heart out. Fight your heart out, Prince.'

Dust like dry ice around their feet
As Hector draws away
Onto and up the rise above the well, three spearcasts now
Above the Skéan Road
Beside him, Ábassee, Chylábborak, T'lespiax,
Swish go their 18-inchers, swish,
Behind T'lespiax, Bóran, his instrumentalists,
Their silver-cuffed black oxhorns poised.

The Child is almost up to them:

'Front for a family of thieves!
No fouler being than a treacherous guest!'

His masks
Slipping and slithering up the bloodstained rise.
'Who needs Achilles now?' calls Déckalin
(An eight-foot maceman from Arcadia)
Within a long jump of the Prince, who
Sweeping his spear detectorwise
Put Déckalin between the Child and himself,
Finessed his sweep into an upwards thrust:
– 'Nice one!' –
That Déckalin (who saw himself – once home –
Beneath a tree, a drink in hand, describing Troy
Its wonders and its wealth) took on his noseguard's bridge.

Well manufactured as the helmet was
The spearpoint penetrated Déckalin's skull
And spurts of blood and bits of brain
Came through its tortoise holes.
    And as the maceman's ghost stumped off,
Diomed:
    '...Yes...'
Watched for a chance to send the Prince
Gone Déckalin's body weighing down his spear
Into Oblivion
    'Yes...' as
Hooking his posy shield
Onto a finger of his spear-arm's hand
Hector signed:
    Advance to Boran and
    '... patience now...'
Raising their ox-horns to their lips
The trio sent a long deep even note
Over that dreadful world;
So otherwise it brought a pause; and in that pause
From either outskirt of the slope
The masses at its centre saw
Bronze beams tanning the dusty sky
And heard – the Child still eyeing Hector,
Hector still stuck with Déckalin on his spear –
Aeneas and Sarpédon's multitudes
    'Wait for it...'
Cheering far off as they advanced.
    'He is bound to show his throat...' Then
    'Yes!'
As Déckalin slid off,
As, Child, you took the breath to power your cast,
    He did
    And lord Idomeneo's fingers ringed your wrist
And lord Odysseus, thwarting Hector's plan, said –

'Who gives a toss what lord Odysseus said?' you said,
Offing the Cretan's grip:
    'Kill...' and aimed your spear '...my kill'
Hop-stumbling-forwards, watching it arc:
    'And I will you.'

Not your day, Dio, not your day.

    Jump from Aeneas' right
Hooves thundering in the dust
Cool-Heart-Boy-Lutie turned his bodice and his pair
Into the flight-path of your spear
Which pierced that urn
Then knocked him black back flat
Out of the car onto the sand
Further from Hector than from you
Longing to kill the Boy
Crying: 'Die! Die!' among the depth of cries
Idomeneo getting in your way,
Friendly – as we go tight – Odysseus's:
    'King,
Come to the ridge.
Hector has pulled you, plus a third of us –'

– 'And I shall kill him as he pulls.' –

Odysseus – that smile of his.

And then, still far, yet louder now,
The outskirts' cheer, the outskirts' dust.

Sethynos says: 'Son of Tydéus, go or stay.
I am your next. If you die, I die. Choose.'

23

He hates to. He is loyal. They have gone.

    And Hector's plan
(Albeit he got his Lutie back)
Is gone.

    Host must fight host,
And to amuse the Lord our God
Man slaughter man.

The sea.
The city on its eminence.
The snow.
And where King Agamemnon drew his sword
And all Greece drew soon after seven today,
Flat, broad, declining stripwards, and
Double the width of Troy,
The ridge.

King Agamemnon sees Mount Ida's vines.
And that is all that he or Greece can see
Save for a coast of sunlit dust
Travelling upslope.

Miss Heber's Diary: 1908. Mid-June.
'We made our way through rain so thick
The midday light was as at home at dusk.
Then, suddenly, the downpour ceased, and there,
A thousand yards across, silent before our feet,
The great gold glittering Limpopo swept towards its Falls.'

So Greece saw Troy exit its dust.
But heroes are not frightened by appearances.
'Ave!' we called.
'Our banners rising one by one
One after one accepting their advance.
Our kings delighting You
Dear Lord and Master of the Widespread Sky
With battle cries. Your cry:
Strike now. As one. And you will win.

Our cry, as we, urns close, our masks like ripples on a lake,
Lowered our spearheads and prepared to fight.'

Troy silent. Slow. The dust
Wreathing up lazily behind their coffin-tops.

AGAMEMNON/MENELAOS

ODYSSEUS	THOAL	NESTOR	DIOMED	AJAX	CRETE

And those who follow them
Watch

SARPÉDON	GRAY	CHYLÁBBORAK	AENEAS	ÁBASSEE

THE PRINCE

This is the moment when you understand
That there is nothing in between
You and the enemy.
Too soon
You may be lying, one life less, seeing the past,
Or standing over someone you have known
Since childhood (or never known) beseeching you
To finish them,
Or on the run,
Or one of those who blindfold those who run,
Or one of those who learn to love it all.

THE PRINCE

(Glancing towards T'lespiax:)

'Forgotten kings
Put down your arms, run to your ships, launch them by dark

26

Or I will turn them into firewood.
And – '
And as he said so, Atreus, shouting:
'God for Greece!'
Floated the opening spear.

All in a moment on T'lespiax' note
10,000 javelins rose into the air
Catching the light but shadowing the ground
That lay between the enemies
    As Greece
Masks down, points down, in body-paint, in bronze
Beating their shields to trumpet drums and stunt-hoop
        tambourines
Advanced onto that ground
    While on T'lespiax' second note
Prince Hector's line of shield-fronts opened up
    – As Greece increased its pace –
To let their balaclavas led by Hux
(Who gave a farm the size of Texas for Cassandra)
Fender their scaffold pike-heads into Greece,
    As Greece:
    'Ave!'
    Now at a run
Came on through knee-deep dust beneath
Flight after flight from Teucer's up-ridge archers as:
    'Slope shields!'
    'Slope shields!'
The Trojan lords shout to their ranks,
And take the shock.

    Think of the moment when far from the land
    Molested by a mile-a-minute wind

The ocean starts to roll, then rear, then roar
Over itself in rank on rank of waves
Their sides so steep their smoky crests so high
300,000 plunging tons of aircraft carrier
Dare not sport its beam.
But Troy, afraid, yet more afraid
Lest any lord of theirs should notice any one of them
Flinching behind his mask
Has no alternative.
   Just as those waves
    Grown closer as they mount the continental shelf
    Lift into breakers scoop the blue and then
    Smother the glistening shingle
Such is the fury of the Greeks
That as the armies joined
No Trojan lord or less can hold his ground, and
    Hapless as plane-crash bodies tossed ashore
    Still belted in their seats
Are thrust down-slope.

Slip into the fighting.
Into a low-sky site crammed with huge men,
Half-naked men, brave, loyal, fit, slab-sided men,
Men who came face to face with gods, who spoke with gods,
Leaping onto each other like wolves
Screaming, kicking, slicing, hacking, ripping
Thumping their chests:
   'I am full of the god!'
Blubbering with terror as they beg for their lives:
   'Laid his trunk open from shoulder to hip –
Like a beauty-queen's sash.'
Falling falling
Top-slung steel chain-gates slumped onto concrete,

Pipko, Bluefisher, Chuckerbutty, Lox:
  'Left all he had to follow Greece.'
  'Left all he had to follow Troy.'
Clawing the ground calling out for their sons for revenge.

Go left along the ridge. Beneath,
Greek chariots at speed. Their upcurled dust.
  Go low along the battle's seam.
Its suddenly up-angled masks.
  Heading 2000 Greeks Thoal of Calydon
A spear in one a banner in his other hand
Has pinched Sarpédon's Lycians in a loop.

  Drop into it.
Noise so clamorous it sucks.
You rush your pressed-flower hackles out
To the perimeter.
  And here it comes:
That unpremeditated joy as you
– The Uzi shuddering warm against your hip
Happy in danger in a dangerous place
Yourself another self you found at Troy –
Squeeze nickel through that rush of Greekoid scum!
Oh wonderful, most wonderful, and then again more wonderful
A bond no word or lack of words can break,
Love above love!
  And here they come again the noble Greeks,
Ido, a spear in one a banner in his other hand
Your life at every instant up for –
Gone.
  And, candidly, who gives a toss?
Your heart beats strong. Your spirit grips.
King Richard calling for another horse (his fifth).

King Marshal Ney shattering his sabre on a cannon ball.
King Ivan Kursk, 22.30 hrs,
July 4th to 14th '43, 7000 tanks engaged,
'... he clambered up and pushed a stable-bolt
Into that Tiger-tank's red-hot-machine-gun's mouth
And bent the bastard up. Woweee!'
Where would we be if he had lost?
Achilles? Let him sulk.

Back to today.
    At the loop's midpoint in the rising dust,
Continual drifts of arrowshafts and stones
Lessening their light, the kings of Lycia:
Sarpédon, Gray, Hágnet, Anáxapart
Silent and sorrowful.
    And queuing to that point lord Hágnet's followers
Raising their voices in farewell,
Each carrying, unasked, though under fire
The biggest stone that he can lift.
    'Oh, we have lost him,'
    'Oh, we have lost him,'
Then placing it
Onto the cairn those first in line have raised
Over their King, lord Hágnet's father, Bárbarinth
Who fell with honour where he fell seven times hit
Dust in his curls far from his home in Aphrodísias
Yet would not give a fingerslength of Hector's ridge to Greece
    Hector himself
Joining the queue adding his stone to theirs
    Taking Sarpédon's hand in his
Shouting above the noise:
    – 'When I have finished with the Greeks
Lord Hágnet shall have Crete.'

30

– 'Don't let me keep you, then.'
But he has gone, Lutie on reins across the battle's back.

Hay and manure, some pools of blood.
They look towards the centre of the ridge. It's dust, like trees.
   Aeneas says:
   'Delay. The day depends on you.'
   Hector: 'On God.'
   'Lock onto them. Exhaust them. Hope they charge.'

Oh, but they do!

The mid-ridge fighting is so intermixed
Its thousands heave, then rear, and then
Collapse back on themselves but cannot part.

   Hector is everywhere, the army king
Now moving pausing now now moving on,
The big bridge of his shoulders everywhere
His mittens flickering in the dusty light
His vulture plume the tallest plume the plume that says:
'Hector is here for anyone at anytime to find and fight to death.'
As he hacks his way on foot towards Chylábborak.

   Drums in the dust. Inside its mid-ridge overcast
Flags tossing above agitated forms.
   Chylábborak, holding the centre firm.
Blurred bronze. Blood? Blood like a car-wash:
   'But it keeps the dust down.'

Each time Greece drew its breath and smashed,
And smash they came and smash they came and smashed and
        smashed
Their eights into the line of coffin-tops,
Across the half-shield-high eye-tingling dust
Prince Hector's voice reached right reached left
And in them both both heart and voices raised
That reached and raised in turn Chylábborak's hearts.
Chylábborak calliing:
    'Greece, is this the best that you can do?
Try harder, Greece.'

Oh, but they do!

Bow your head. Beg for your life. Death without burial.
And there – as if
    Inside a moonlit sandstorm God allowed
    The columns of Palmýra speech –
The Greeks encouraging their host:
    'I am here. I will help.
Stand still and fight. At any moment they will break.'
Though they do not.

    Chylábborak:
    'Greece, are you frightened?
Why come so far to die?' and unbelievably
Feeling the cobbles of the Skéan Road beneath his feet.
    And still –
    As one sits upright from a dream in which he drowned
    And reaches for the light –
Troy reached inside itself and found new strength,

Though Greece –
    Like a pedestrian who thinks: 'After this hill, downhill,'
    Then from its top sees yet another hill –
Kept coming back:
    'Yet some who looked our way would sigh for us.'

    Back from the dust, in quarter light
Masks up, bronze off, arms up, water dashed round
Happy to see each other through the dust,
Kykéon at his father's side,
Chylábborak shouts to Hector:
    'Even if I say so – which I do – our centre holds.'
A nod.
    'But it is not enough to lock/exhaust them.
They must be driven back.
And only you can make us do it.
Only you.'

    Kykéon smiles. He is Prince Hector's nephew. When
– As is the practice in South Ilium –
They estimate how long a boy's first spear should be
That year's cadets lie on their backs reach back an arm
And hope to lift the spear whose butt their fathers lay
Across their palms, in one smooth swing.
Kykéon (8) lifted a 10-foot spear, that Hector swapped
For his first (also ten) – its spearhead socket with a golden rim.

Impacted battle. Dust above a herd.
Hands wielding broken spearpoles rise through ice-hot twilight
        flecked with points.
    And where you end and where the dust begins
Or if it is the dust or men that move
And whether they are Greek or Trojan, well

Only this much is certain: when a lull comes – they do –
You hear the whole ridge coughing.

   'There's Bubblegum!' 'He's out to make his name!'
'He's charging us!' 'He's prancing!' 'Get that leap!'
   THOCK! THOCK!
'He's in the air!' 'Bubblegum's in the air!' 'Above the dust!'
'He's lying on the sunshine in the air!' 'Seeing the Wall!' 'The
      arrows keep him up!'
   THOCK! THOCK!
'Olé!' 'He's wiggling in the air!' 'They're having fun with him!'
'He's saying something!' 'Bubblegum's last words!'
'He's down!' 'He's in the dust!' 'Bubblegum's in the dust!'
'They're stripping him!' 'They're stripping Bubblegum!'
   'Close!'
   'Close!'
   'You can't see anything!'
   'His mother sold her doves to buy his plate!'
   'You can't see who to kill!'

   Sunlight like lamplight.
Brown clouds of dust touch those brown clouds of dust already
      overhead.
And snuffling through the blood and filth-stained legs
Of those still-standing-thousands goes
Nasty, Thersites' little dog,
Now licking this, now tasting that.

   Nestor, his son, Antilochus, standing beside him:

   'Belovéd friends:
This stasis is God's work:
And it is blasphemous to win when He says wait...'

34

Hector is on his knees:

'Bringer of Daylight
Lord of Mice and Light
Help me to drive the Greeks
Into the sea.'

On Agamemnon's right, the Child,
Due to put on 10 years and lose 10lbs this afternoon:
　'We are Greek! We are brave! Add your strength to mine!'

As Lord Apollo answered Hector's prayer:

'Believer –
You are handsome, you are loved,
Bursting with hope and possibility,
Unyielding, ever-active, dangerous, true.
But no man can do everything alone.'
　'Speak out, speak up,
And I will help you drive the kings of Greece
Over the plain, across Scamánder, through the palisade
Into the shadow of their ships.'

'All souls!'
– You feel the god in Hector's voice –
'You are magnificent.
　Magnificent,
From Thrace, from Bosphorous, from Anatólium,
From Caran Lycia, from Phrýgiland,
Cyprus and Simi, Sámothrace and Cos,
　Magnificent,
My heroes and my host of Ilium.
　Now let us finish with the Greeks,

35

And drive them off this ridge that they pollute,
And chase them down the plain that they have scorched
And into the Scamánder they have soured.
And slaughter them beside their bloated ships.
    Founded by Heaven, founded in Heaven,
You of the never taken Gate to Asia, Holy Troy,
Rouse your brave hearts! Do as I do! Do as I say! Kill Greece!
The victory is God's! The victory –'
As with a downward sweep of his arm
Boy Lutie lashed their pair –
    'Is God's!'
And drove his Prince, his lord, his love, Hector of Troy,
T'lespiax trumpeting:
    'The victory –'
With 50 chariots on either side,
And running by their wheels, all answering his:
    'Is God's!'
    'Is God's!'
His mass
Followed him through the swathes of hanging dust.

Sparks from the bronze. Lit splinters from the poles.
'I am hit.'
'Take my arm.'
'I am dying.'
'Shake my hand.'
'Do not go.'
'Goodbye little fellow with the gloomy face.'
As Greece, as Troy, fought on and on.

    Or are they only asleep?
They are too tired to sleep.
The tears are falling from their eyes.

36

The noise they make while fighting is so loud
That what you see is like a silent film.
And as the dust converges over them
The ridge is as it is when darkness falls.

Silence and light.

The earth
And its attendant moon
(Neither of great importance
But beautiful and dignified)
Making their way around the sun.

Bread trucks have begun to stream
across the vast plateau,
fair skies, high cumulus cloud –
the birds are in full throat
as the sun lights up the east.
Who is it sees
Set in the north Aegean sea, their coasts
Nosegays of seaweed toasting Ida's snow,
The Isles of Imbros and of Sámothrace?
And over there – grapes ghosts and vocal grottoes –
Greece. Above it, Mácedon,
Its wooded folds declining till they meet
Those of Carpáthia at the Kágan Gorge,
Through which, fed by a hundred tributaries since
It crossed the northern instep of the Alps,
The Danube reappears.
Eyes onto Italy
(Where squirrels go from coast to coast and never touch the ground)

Then up, over her cyclorama peaks
Whose snow became before the fire before the wheel, the Rhine,
Below whose estuaries beneath an endless sky,
Sand bars and sabre grass, salt flats and travelling dunes
Lead west, until, green in their shallow sea
That falls away into the Atlantic deeps
He sees the Islands of the West.
    He who? Why, God, of course.
Who sighs before He looks
Back to the ridge that is, save for a million footprints,
Empty now.

Notes

page

14   *'I shall be busy ...'*: cf. Sir Jacob Astley's prayer before the battle of Edgehill (Warick, *Memoires*, 1701).

18   'Blind as the Cyclops with fraternal tears': cf. Dryden's 'Astraea Redux', l. 45.

19   'Blends with the sound' to 'circled by poplar trees'. Jasper Griffin's translation from Virgil's *Georgics*.

25   'The great gold glittering Limpopo': cf. Rudyard Kipling's *The Jungle Book*, 'The Elephant's Child' – 'The great, green, greasy Limpopo'.

27   'All in a moment on T'lespiax' note': cf. Milton's *Paradise Lost*, I, 544.

28   ' "I am full of the god!" ': cf. Pope's *Iliad*, XIII, 115.

29   'Oh wonderful, most wonderful, and then again more wonderful': cf. *As You Like It*, III, ii, 202.

30   The lines from 'King Ivan Kursk ...' to '... if he had lost?' derive from John Erickson's *The Road to Berlin: Stalin's War with Germany*, vol. 2, and from Boris Slutsky's *Things that Happened* (poems and notes), translated with commentaries by G. S. Smith.

31   'Flags tossing above agitated forms': cf. Stephen Crane, *The Red Badge of Courage*.

34   ' "There's Bubblegum!" ': this passage derives from the opening pages of Louis-Ferdinand Céline's *Guignol's Band*, translated by Bernard Frechtman and Jack T. Nile.

37   The lines: 'Bread trucks have begun to stream' to 'as the sun lights up the east' are from August Kleinzahler's poem 'An Englishman Abroad'.